Cookbook

of the

Congregational Church

(Stone Church)

Methuen, Mass.

1927

SicPress 2013
Methuen, MA

Originally published by the First Congregational Church, Methuen, Mass 1927.

Detail from the original pastel painting "Rose of Sharon" by Sharon Morley, APS - sharonmorley.com

©2013 SicPress.com
14 Pleasant St.
Methuen, Massachusetts.
sales@sicpress.com

RECIPES

Meats

"Don't talk all the talk, nor eat all the meat" —Proverb

HAM BAKED IN MILK
Get a slice of ham 1½ inches thick. Lay flat in a casserole. Mix 1 level tablesp. sugar with 1 teasp. dry mustard. Spread on top of ham and rub in with back of spoon. Cover ham with milk and bake in moderate oven 2 hours.
MRS. HATTIE A. WARDWELL

FILLING FOR CHICKEN PATTIES FOR FIFTY
Piece of butter size of a large walnut; put in double boiler; when melted stir in ½ cup pastry flour a little at a time. Skim fat from chicken stock, warm the stock and pour into flour and butter, stirring all the time. Season with salt, celery salt, paprika and a little onion juice. Add three pounds of meat of chicken cut fine. Add three bottles of thin cream. Use about 2 quarts of stock for this recipe. Makes enough for 50 pattie shells.
MRS. CHARLES. E. RUSSELL

HUNGARIAN GOULASH
Cook 1 cup of Maccaroni in salted boiling water until tender. Saute 1 onion and cook with 1 pound Hamburg Steak, salt and pepper. Then add 1 can of tomato soup and the Maccaroni.
MAUDE A. IRISH

WELSH RABBIT
Mix together with a little water ½ Teasp. Mustard, ½ Teasp. Salt, ½ Teasp. Flour. Break into this 1 egg and beat. Add one cup of milk and beat again.
Pour this into blazer over hot water pan, that has a little melted melted butter in it. Add 1 lb. unmelted cheese and cook together until cheese is melted. Beat until creamy with egg beater.
MRS. L. H. CONANT

RECIPES

FANCY OMELET

4 Eggs, 1 tablesp. milk or water, ½ Teasp. salt, dash pepper, two teasps. butter, separate yolks and whites of eggs. Beat yolks until creamy, add seasoning and milk or water. Beat whites stiff and cut and fold them into yolk mixture.

MRS. L. H. CONANT

CHEESE SOUFFLE'

2 tablesp. butter; 3 tablesp. flour; ½ cup scalded milk; ½ teasp. salt; bit of cayenne; ½ cup grated cheese; 3 eggs. Melt butter, add flour and when well mixed add milk gradually. Then add salt. cayenne, and cheese. Remove from fire, add beaten yolks to mixture and fold in beaten whites. Pour into buttered baking dish and bake 20 minutes in slow oven (325°F) **Serve at once.**

MRS. HATTIE A. WARDWELL

PORK CHOPS EN CASSEROLE

Saute 6 or 8 chops until browned on both sides. Put in casserole on a bed of vegetables (onions, potatoes and carrots may be used) add water to cover add ½ teaspoon salt. Cover tightly and cook in oven two hours. When ready to serve, thicken the stock.

EDITH GOLDSMITH

VEGETABLE TURKEY

1 cup chopped English walnuts, 1 cup bread crumbs, 1 cup Milk, 1 Egg, 1 Teasp. turkey seasoning, ½ Teasp. salt.
Soak nuts and bread in milk a few minutes. Add egg and seasoning. Bake about half an hour in small loaf. Serve hot with tomato sauce, or cold in place of meat.

MRS. ROLF NORRIS

BEEF LOAF

One lb. fresh beef, 1 lb. fresh pork, 6 Uneeda biscuits, 2 eggs, 2 teaspoonfuls of salt, ¼ teaspoonful of pepper, ½ cup of milk. Put meat through chopper, roll biscuits fine, drop eggs unbeaten-- mix all thoroughly—put in baking tin. Bake one hour.

MRS. SPICER

RECIPES

FRICANDOS
1 cup chopped cooked cold meat (lamb and beef mixed,) 1 cup fine bread crumbs, 1 sweet pepper chopped, 1 beaten egg, dash of curry, celery salt, parsley, salt and pepper. Mould in cakes, brown in butter. Sauce for same: 1 tablespoon butter, 1 tablespoon flour, 1 tablespoon tomato ketsup, 1 tablespoon quarts of stock for this recipe. Makes enough for 50 pattie Worcestershire sauce, and stock or water to thin.

MRS. H. E. MOORE

OVEN STEW
2 lbs. lean round steak cut in squares as for beef tea, 4 medium sized potatoes cut in slices, 1 carrot cut in slices, pepper, salt. Take large bean pot, butter inside, then put in meat, add teaspoonful flour sifted over meat, then add potatoes, onions, carrot, seasoning, another teaspoon of sifted flour, fill pot with cold water and cover tight. Put in oven and cook a number of hours. It will be done in 4 hours, but is better if cooked longer. Keep it filled with water

MRS. J. A. EMERSON

BEEF STEW
Into 2 pounds of round steak pound 1 cup of flour. Fry in pork or bacon fat. Cover with water and simmer, add onion, carrot and tomato, salt, pepper; simmer 3 or 4 hours, or cook in fireless cooker 6 hours.

DR. AGNES FRASER

MUTTON CHOPS, BREADED
Trim the chops, make them into a circle and secure with wooden toothpicks. Score the edges and sprinkle with pepper and salt. Dip in bread crumbs, then in beaten egg, then in bread crumbs again and fry in boiling fat. Arrange on hot platter, garnish with parsley and pour around it tomato sauce.

MRS. HELEN SPOONER

TOMATO SAUCE
1 pint tomatoes, ½ onion, 4 cloves. Cook 15 minutes. Melt 1 tablespoon butter, brown, add 1 tablespoon flour, salt and pepper to taste. Cook 2 minutes. Rub through sieve.

MRS. HELEN SPOONER

RECIPES

MEAT SCALLOP

Layers of chopped meat, with little pepper and salt; then bread crumbs and bits of butter. Over all pour 2 eggs beaten in 1 cup milk. Bake ½ hour in hot oven. Corn scallop made in same way.

MRS. H. A. DODGE

TURKISH PILAF

⅓ cup Rice, cooked and cold, 3 tablespoons Butter, ½ cup canned Tomatoes, ½ to 1 cup cold cooked Chicken, cut in small pieces, white stock. Heat frying pan, add butter; as soon as melted add rice, cook three minutes, then add tomatoes, chicken and enough stock to moisten. Cook five minutes, season with salt and cayenne. Lamb may be used instead of the chicken

MRS. AMY GREENE

TURKEY OR CHICKEN SOUFFLE

Melt 2 tablespoons Butter, add 2 tablespoons Flour, when smooth pour in gradually 1 pint hot, rich Milk, and stir until smooth; add one pint of Turkey or Chicken chopped fine, season to taste and cook gently for 5 minutes, then stir in the beaten yolks of 3 Eggs, remove from fire and cool. Beat whites till they can be cut with a knife, fold lightly into the meat and turn into the meat and turn into a buttered, thin baking dish, and bake in a hot oven for 20 minutes.

MRS. STEPHEN E. SMITH

BAKED HAM

Slice of Ham, put in baking pan, cover with Milk, bake 45 minutes, remove ham, thicken gravy with 1 desert spoon of flour.

MRS. SPICER

HAM AND MACARONI SCALLOP

Cook sufficient macaroni to make 1 pint, mince ⅔ as much ham, put in alternate layers in a baking dish, season with a little pepper and mustard and moisten well with white sauce. 2 or 3 hard boiled eggs sliced, may be added if convenient. Cover the top with a layer of buttered crumbs, and bake about half an hour, or until brown.

MRS. HARRY H. JOHNSON

RECIPES

BREAKFAST DISH
Chop a cupful of ham, boiled or fried, put tablespoon of butter in hot spider, add ham, stir till hot, then break over it as many eggs as needed, add pepper and stir until eggs are set.
MRS. S. B. CARROW

HAM PATTIES
1 part ham, boiled or fried, chop fine, 2 parts bread crumbs wet with milk, mix, put in gem pans, break one egg over each, sprinkle with crumbs and bake brown.
MRS. S. B. CARROW

MINT SAUCE
Mix 3 tablespoons finely chopped mint with 1 tablespoon brown sugar and one tea cup vinegar, let stand 10 minutes.
MRS. CARRIE E. BARNES

Vegetables and Entrees
"The discovery of a new dish does more for the happiness of man than the discovery of a new star."
Brillat Savasin

PARSNIPS
Boil the parsnips, mash, add butter, salt, pepper and form into cakes, roll in flour and fry in butter until brown.
MRS. S. B. CARROW

CORN FRITTERS
2 eggs, one cup milk, ½ can corn, 1 teaspoon Royal baking powder, salt, 1 tablespoon sugar, 2 tablespoons butter, flour.
MRS. SUSIE J. MANN — MRS. SWAIN

FRUIT FRITTERS
1 egg, ½ cup milk, heaping teaspoon Royal baking powder, salt, scant cup flour, stir in two apples, chopped fine. Drop from spoon into hot lard and fry. Peaches, pineapple or any desired fruit may be used. Serve with sauce like steamed pudding sauce.
MRS. HENRY GAUNT

TOMATOES A LA NEWBURG
Cream together in double boiler 1 tablespoon butter, 2 tablespoons flour, add 1 pint tomato juice, 1 lb. cheese, salt and pepper to taste, serve hot on saltines.
MRS. GEORGE TENNEY

RECIPES

CHEESE CROQUETTES

Make a thick sauce using 3 tablespoons butter, ¼ cup flour and ⅔ milk. Add yolks of 2 eggs and stir until mixed, then add in one cup mild cheese cut in small cubes. Season with salt. ½ cup grated Grauyer's cheese. As soon as cheese melts fold pepper and cayenne. Spread on plate to cool. Shape, dip in crumbs, egg and crumbs and fry in deep fat.

MRS. FREDERICK GAY

CHEESE TOAST

Make a cream sauce of 1 heaping tablespoon each of butter and flour and one cup milk, add a cup of grated cheese, season with salt and a few grains of cayenne pepper. Toast bread carefully, trim and butter, pour over the cheese sauce and serve immediately.

DR. AGNES FRASER

CHEESE PUDDING

1 cup cheese cut fine, 1 cup bread crumbs, 1½ cups milk, 1 beaten egg, ½ teaspoon salt, ½ teaspoon mustard, dash of cayenne pepper, bake in moderate oven 30 minutes and serve at once.

MRS. HARRY H. JOHNSON

RICE CHEESE

1 cup boiled rice, 1 cup grated cheese, 1 beaten egg. Cream sauce made of 2 tablespoons butter, 2 tablespoons flour 1 cup milk. Season to taste with salt and a few grains cayenne pepper. Mix, put into buttered baking dish or ramekins, cover with buttered crumbs and bake 20 minutes.

DR. AGNES FRASER

CHEESE PATTIES

½ cup cheese, rather strong, ½ teaspoon salt, ¼ teaspoon pepper, ½ teaspoon mustard, 1 tablespoon flour, 1 egg, 1 cup milk. Cook in double boiler until thick, serve on soda crackers or in shredded wheat baskets.

MISS EDITH GOLDSMITH

SYRUP FOR FRITTERS

1 cup white sugar, 1 cup brown sugar, 1 cup boiling water, stir and boil 3 minutes, ½ teaspoon vanilla.

MRS. P. C. COOK

RECIPES

CRUST PATTIES

From a loaf of stale bread cut slices an inch and a half thick, with a patty cutter cut out as many rounds as desired, press half through each piece with a smaller cutter. Place in a frying basket and plunge into boiling fat until brown, about half a minute. Place on a paper with a napkin over to absorb every particle of fat. Remove centre cover and take out soft bread underneath, fill, and put on covers.

FILLING FOR CRUSTS

Put two tablespoons of butter in the frying pan and when melted add 1 of flour, stir until smooth, add one cup of milk and boil one minute. Stir in 1 pint of oysters, chicken, lobster or veal, season with pepper and salt. Fill the crusts, place on hot platter covered with napkin.

MRS. C. H. OLIPHANT

TENDERLOIN FILLING FOR PATTIES

2 oz. butter, 2 tablespoons flour, blend in double boiler, add 1 pt. cream, pinch cayenne pepper, little salt, **speck** of nutmeg, cook until it thickens. Cut a few slices of tenderloin into dice, blanch in boiling water, cook 20 minutes or until tender, add to cream.

MR. A. B. DAVIS

SALMON WIGGLE

1 pint thick cream sauce, well cooked. Add 1 beaten egg and dash of cayenne pepper. Stir well and add ½ can salmon, ½ can peas. Serve hot on toast or crackers.

CHICKEN WIGGLE

Same as above using chicken instead of salmon.

RUTH NORRIS

BAKED FISH WITH CHEESE

4-lb. haddock, schrodded. Butter large flat pan. Lay in fish, skin side down, and sprinkle salt, dust of pepper, and 1 cup cheese sliced thin or grated. Add 1½ cups milk. Bake in oven 30 minutes at 400° F. When done, remove fish and thicken gravy.

MRS. HATTIE A. WARDWELL

RECIPES

Salads

"To make a perfect salad there should be a spendthrift for oil, a miser for vinegar, a wise man for salt, and a madcap to stir the ingredients up and mix them well together.   —Spanish Proverb

SALAD DRESSING (Parker House Rule)

4 eggs, 2 dessertspoons sugar, 8 tablespoons (½ cup) olive oil, 1 tablespoon salt, 2 tablespoons mixed mustard, ½ cup vinegar, speck of cayenne pepper. Beat eggs and sugar together; add oil, a little at a time; add other ingredients. Put cayene in vinegar to prevent lumps. When all is well mixed strain into double boiler and cook like soft custard, stirring **all** the time. When cold add 1 bottle of thick cream which has been whipped. This (bottled) will keep for one year. If it thickens from time to time add more cream.

MRS. M. A. BUSWELL

MAYONNAISE

1 tablespoon mustard, 1 tablespoon sugar, 1 teaspoon salt, ½ teaspoon pepper, mixed; yolks of 3 eggs, 1 cup oil, 1 cup butter, ¼ cup vinegar, ½ lemon (juice) 1 cup cream or milk, last add the beaten whites of eggs.

MRS. GEORGE TENNEY

RED MAYONNAISE

1 cup of mayonnaise dressing, 1 cup of thick tomato sauce, 1 cup whipped cream. Have the tomato sauce hot and pour it boiling over the mayonnaise, beating vigorously, and then set in ice water. Add the beaten cream.

MRS. GEORGE TENNEY

RECIPES

SALAD DRESSING

Sift together 2 level tablespoons of sugar, 2 level tablespoons of cornstarch, 1 teaspoon of mustard, add to 2 beaten eggs. When thoroughly mixed pour into double boiler containing 1 pint scalded milk. Cook 13 minutes, stirring constantly. Take from fire and beat in 1 cup vinegar and ½ cup olive oil (or 1 tablespoon of butter) and 1 teaspoon salt.

MRS. B. L. BARSTOW
MRS. J. A. EMERSON

SALAD DRESSING

1 heaping teaspoon mustard, ½ teaspoon salt, ½ teaspoon sugar. Mix with little hot water. 1 tablespoon melted butter dropped drop by drop into above mixture. 2 eggs beaten very light, turn slowly into mixture, 1/3 cup of milk or cream, 1/3 cup cold vinegar. Mix well, set in bowl over tea kettle, and cook until thick.

MRS. D. D. WOODBURY

CABBAGE SALAD

3 eggs, 1 tablespoon mustard, 1 tablespoon sugar, 1 tablespoon salt, 1 tablespoon butter, 1 cup milk, 1 cup vinegar. Beat the eggs very light, add to the dry ingredients, put in double boiler, add milk, when warm add vinegar, boil until consistency of thick cream. Shave cabbage with sharp knife, add layer of cabbage, layer of dressing, cover with plate; letting it stand over night improves flavor.

MRS. M. E. DORWARD

SALAD DRESSING FOR FRUIT SALAD

1 cup sugar, yolk of 1 egg, 1 lemon beat thoroughly and add just before serving, ½ bottle of cream. Serves 8 people.

MRS. W. A. GABELER

RECIPES

SALAD OF PEPPERS AND CREAM CHEESE

Two large, green peppers, cut off stem and remove seeds, wash and drain. 2 cream cheeses, mash, and mix into them chopped walnuts or pecan nuts, fill the peppers very solid and cool on ice. Cut in slices and serve on a lettuce leaf, add a few slices of cucumber and mayonnaise dressing.

MISS FAIRFIELD

FRUIT SALAD DRESSING

Heat together in double boiler ¼ cup pineapple juice, ¼ cup lemon juice ¼ cup orange juice. Add 2 eggs, beaten light, ½ cup sugar, ½ tablespoon cornstarch. Cook like custard, beat until cold, fold in ½ cup heavy cream. Enough for ten.

MRS. BAKETEL

BOILED SALAD DRESSING

Mix together in double boiler and cook until it thickens ½ Tablespoon mustard, ⅓ Tablespoon salt, 1 big tablespoon sugar, 1 egg, 1 heaping tablespoon flour, 2 big tablespoons melted butter, ¼ cup vinegar, 1 cup milk.

MRS. GERTRUDE KING

MY FAVORITE SALAD DRESSING

1 teaspoon mustard, 1 teaspoon salt; pour on 1 cup vinegar. Then add 1 can Eagle Brand Condensed Milk and beat with egg beater. 2 eggs (beaten) and beat in. Add 12 cent jar Blue Ribbon Mayonnaise, a speck of red pepper. No cooking, and keeps indefinitely.

MRS. HATTIE A. WARDWELL

EGG AND POTATO SALAD

Dice 3 cold boiled potatoes and cover with above dressing 2 hours before serving. Just before serving add 3 hard boiled eggs diced. This will serve 4.

MRS. HATTIE A. WARDWELL

RECIPES

Puddings

"The proof of the pudding is in the eating" —Cervantes

INDIAN PUDDING

1 quart milk, ¼ cup suet, ¼ cup butter, 5 tablespoons Indian meal. Scald 1 pint of milk and add Indian meal and suet. To remainder of milk add 1 egg, 1 tablespoon flour, 1 teacup molasses, 1 teaspoon ginger, 1 cup raisins. Mix all together and bake **slowly** three or four hours.

MRS. C. A. GOLDSMITH

INDIAN TAPIOCA PUDDING

1 qt. milk, 2 large spoonsful Indian meal, 4 dessertspoonsful tapioca, scald together until thick, add 1 egg, ½ teacup molasses, ½ teacup sugar, very little ginger, ⅛ or ¼ teaspoosful; ¼ teaspoonful cassia, little salt, bake from 1 to 1½ hours.

MARION CROSBY

HEAVENLY HASH

Whip a jar of heavy cream, crush four bananas, cut in quarters 7 or 8 marshmallows, put marshmallows and bananas in cream, flavor with vanilla, put chopped nuts and cherry on top. Serve in sherbert glasses.

MRS. STOWELL

GRAPENUT PUDDING

1 egg well beaten, ⅔ cup grapenut, 1 pint milk, ½ cup sugar, ⅔ cup prunes, stewed and stoned. Salt to taste. Slice butter over top before baking. Bake 1 hour. Serve cold with thick or whipped cream.

ADELAIDE S. KAY

COFFEE SOUFFLE

Heat 1½ cups clear strong coffee, ½ cup milk, ¼ box of Cox gelatine in double boiler. When the milk is hot add ⅔ cup sugar, ¼ teaspoon salt, yolks of 3 eggs. Cook like custard. When cool add beaten whites of eggs and one teaspoon vanilla. Put on ice to harden and serve with cream, whipped.

MRS. THOMAS TRIPP

RECIPES

CRANBERRY PUDDING

1 cup sugar and 3 tablespoons butter, creamed; 1 cup milk, 2¼ cups flour and 2 teaspoons cream tartar, sifted together, 1 teaspoon soda, pinch of salt. Bake in buttered tin ½ hour. Eat with foamy sauce. Cherries may be used instead of cranberries.
MRS. B. W. LIBBY

PEQUOT PUDDING

¼ cup granulated tapioca, 2 tablespoons corn meal, ¼ cup cocoanut 1 teapsoon salt, 1 cup brown sugar, 1 quart of milk. Cook in double boiler until thickened, then bake in oven 1 hour.
MAUDE A. IRISH

DATE CREAM PUDDING

1 pint milk, 1 small cup sugar, yolks 3 eggs, pinch of salt, 1 tablespoon gelatine soaked in 2 tablespoons cold water, 1 cup whipped cream. Put milk, sugar, salt, 3 yolks well beaten into double boiler. Stone and cut 1 lb. dates. When custard begins to thicken stir in dates. Add gelatine. When cool add stiffly beaten whites and cup of whipped cream. Set in cool place to stiffen.
MARION H. TRIPP

PUDDING SAUCE

White of 1 egg beaten stiff, ½ cup powdered sugar, yolk beaten, ½ cup whipped cream. Flavor.
MRS. JENKINSON

QUEEN OF PUDDINGS

1 pint of fine bread crumbs, 1 quart of milk, 1 cup of sugar, yolks of 2 eggs, butter size of an egg. After baking, cover with jam or jelly and add whites of 2 eggs beaten stiff, with ½ cup of sugar. Brown in the oven.
EDITH GOLDSMITH

STEAMED CHOCOLATE PUDDING

1 cup flour, ½ cup sugar, ½ cup milk, 1 egg, ½ teaspoon soda, 1 teaspoon Cream of Tartar, 2 squares chocolate melted with 1 tablespoon butter. Steam 1 hour.

SAUCE

4 tablespoons butter, 8 tablespoons powdered sugar. Cream the above and add 2 beaten whites of eggs. Flavor to taste.
MRS. ROY V. BAKETEL

RECIPES

ENGLISH PLUM PUDDING

3 lbs. flour, 1 lb. Sultanas, 2 lbs. currants, 2 lbs. raisins, 1 lb. candied peel, 2 carrots, 1½ lbs. sugar, 2 oz. allspice, 3 eggs, ½ lb. breadcrumbs, 1 lb. suet, milk enough to mix. Steam 6 hours and 1 before using.

MRS. BAKETEL

CHRISTMAS PLUM PUDDING
(Used over 100 years in the Family)

1 lb. flour, 1 lb. raisins, 1 lb. currants, 1 lb. sugar, ½ lb breadcrumbs, ½ lbs. walnuts, ½ lb. candied peel, 2 lbs. apples, 1 large carrot, ½ lb. suet, 2 eggs, 2 teaspoons salt. Put apples, peel, carrot, suet, walnuts thru meat chopper and mix with 1 cup coffee. 2 Teaspoons cinnamon. Sprinkle clean white cloths with flour and put mixture into each cloth. Tie firmly. Plunge into boiling water. Simmer 5 hours and 1 hour before using. Will keep weeks.

MRS. MATTHEW HARRISON

PLUM PUDDING

3 cups bread flour, 1 cup milk, 1 cup molasses, 1 cup chopped suet, 1 teaspoon soda, salt and each of spices and extracts, ¾ cup raisins. 1 cup citron and orange peel.

MRS. THOMPSON

CARAMEL PUDDING

2 cups brown sugar, 2½ cups hot water. Boil 10 minutes Add 2½ tablespoons cornstarch, wet enough to dissolve, ½ cup chopped nuts, 1 teaspoon vanilla. Let cool. Serve with whipped cream.

MRS. MATTHEW HARRISON

PRUNE PUFF

2 eggs whites, beaten stiff. Add ¼ cup sugar slowly. Add 1 cup prunes which have been stoned and chopped. Whip until light. Bake in pudding dish in moderate oven about 10 minutes. Serve with soft custard.

MRS. WM. ENOS

RECIPES

STEAMED PUDDING

1 egg, 1½ cups sugar, ⅓ cup butter, 1½ cups sour milk, 3 cups flour, 1 teaspoon soda, ½ teaspoon cassia, ¼ teaspoon cloves, 1 cup currants, salt. Steam for 3 hours.

SAUCE: 1 pint milk, ¼ cup sugar, 1 teaspoon heaping corn starch, butter size of English walnut, teaspoon Baker's lemon extract. Cook in double boiler. **Serve hot.**

MRS. HENRY GAUNT

CHRISTMAS PUDDING

¼ lb. citron, ¼ lb. orange and lemon peel, 1 lb. raisins and currants mixed, dust with 6 tablespoons flour, chop ½ lb. suet and add to mixture with ½ lb. stale bread crumbs, ½ nutmeg grated, 2 teaspoons cinnamon, rind and fruit of 1 orange, mix thoroughly, add three eggs, beaten without separating, ½ cup sugar, ½ cup grace juice, mix, pack in mould, boil 6 hours.

SAUCE: 1 cup confectioner's sugar creamed with ½ cup butter, break in unbeaten white of 1 egg, beat together, add a little Baker's vanilla or other flavoring.

MRS. C. H. OLIPHANT

CHRISTMAS PUDDING

Slice a 5c baker's loaf, butter thickly, put in pudding-dish with layers of raisins between slices, 1½ cups raisins. Pour over the bread 1 qt. milk into which has been stirred 4 eggs, 1 cup sugar, 1 saltspoon salt, ½ teaspoon cinnamon, a little clove and nutmeg, let stand 1 hour and then pour or 1 qt. more milk and bake slowly 4 hours.

MRS. D. D. WOODBURY

SUET PUDDING, FOAM SAUCE

1 cup chopped suet, 1 cup raisins, 1 cup Orleans molasses, 1 cup milk, 3 cups flour, little salt and cinnamon, 1 level teaspoon soda, steam 3 hours.

FOAM SAUCE: ½ cup butter, 1 cup powdered sugar, ½ teaspoon Baker's vanilla. Cream all together. Add 2 tablespoons quince or apple jelly and ¼ cup hot water, and beat well.

Just before serving, the beaten white of 1 egg may be added, and beat all together till light and foamy.

MRS. HARVEY S. GRANT

RECIPES

SUET PUDDING
1 cup chopped suet, 1 cup raisins, 1½ cups milk, 1 cup molasses, 3½ cups flour, 1 teaspoon salt, 1 teaspoon spice, 1¼ teaspoons soda, steam 3 hours.

MRS. S. G. SARGENT

CHOCOLATE CUSTARD
1 pint milk, 3½ tablespoons grated chocolate, 1¼ tablespoons corn starch disolved in cold milk, ½ cup sugar, ½ teaspoon vanilla, ½ cup cold milk. Cook in double boiler until it thickens.

MRS. L. H. CONANT

BATTER PUDDING
½ cup sugar, ½ cup milk, 1 egg, 1 teaspoon melted butter, 1 rounded teaspoon Royal baking powder, 1 cup pastry flour. Beat all well and pour over 5 or 6 apples which have been sliced and put in a cake tin or round thin pudding dish.

MRS. HUGH SMITH

NUTMEG PUDDING SAUCE
½ cup butter (scant,) 1 cup sugar, creamed; moisten 2 tablespoonfuls of flour and cook in 1 pint of water till clear like starch, then pour it over the creamed butter and sugar before serving, flavor with nutmeg.

MRS. HUGH SMITH

COTTAGE PUDDING
2 eggs beaten light, 1 cup sugar, 1 cup bread flour sifted with 1 teaspoon (even) Royal Baking Powder, ½ cup hot milk added slowly last. Serve with hot chocolate sauce.

MRS. H. E. MOORE

HOT CHOCOLATE SAUCE
2 level tablespoons butter, 1 cup boiling water, 1 tablespoon flour, 1 square Baker's Chocolate, pinch of salt, 4 level tablespoons sugar, 1 teaspoon Baker's vanilla. Melt butter, add dry flour, and salt and mix till smooth, then slowly add boiling water, beating well, add the chocolate and sugar and stir till melted. Add vanilla just before serving. Good either hot or cold.

MRS. M. A. BUSWELL

RECIPES

MOUNTAIN DEW PUDDING

3 crackers rolled fine, 1 pt. milk, yolks of 2 eggs, small piece of butter, bake; 1 cup sugar added to the whites beaten stiff, put on top and brown.

MRS. H. E. WOODBURY

CHOCOLATE BREAD PUDDING

1 qt. milk, 3 oz. chocolate, 4 eggs, 2 teaspoons Bakers Vanilla, 1½ cup bread crumbs. Bake like custard in pan of hot water. Serve with whipped cream sauce.

MRS. M. A. BUSWELL

STEAMED CHOCOLATE PUDDING

½ cup sugar, 1 tablespoon butter, (melt or not), 1 egg, ½ cup milk, 1 teaspoon Royal Baking Powder, 1 cup flour, 2 squares melted chocolate, steam 1¼ hours.

MRS. M. A. BUSWELL, MRS. H. E. MOORE

HARD SAUCE

1 tablespoon melted butter, 2 tablespoons water (cold,) powdered sugar and make right consistency, teaspoon Baker's vanilla.

MRS. M. A. BUSWELL

WHIPPED CREAM SAUCE

2 eggs, (white and yolks beaten separately), 1 cup powdered sugar, whip ½ cup cream, flavor with Baker's vanilla, add sugar to whites, then add yolks, and add all to whipped cream.

MRS. M. A. BUSWELL

CHOCOLATE PUFF BALLS

A large ½ cup sugar, a large tablespoon butter, 1 egg, ½ cup sweet milk, ½ teaspoon soda, 1 cream tartar, 2 tablespoons cocoa, 1 teaspoon Baker's vanilla, flour enough to make as thick as Johnny cake and steam in cups about 1 hour.
SAUCE: 1 egg, 1 cup sugar beaten to a froth, ½ cup boiling milk, pour in last, flavor with Baker's vanilla.

MRS. GEO. BLODGETT, MRS. SUSIE J. MANN

RECIPES

SNOW BALLS

Cream ¼ cup butter, add ½ cup sugar gradually, ¼ cup milk, add 1⅛ cups flour, mixed and sifted with 1¾ teaspoons Royal Baking Powder, add the whites of 2 eggs beaten stiff. Steam 35 minutes in small buttered moulds. Serve with strawberry sauce.

MRS. A. E. HEALD

A SIMPLE APPLE PUDDING

In a pudding dish put apple sauce about half filling the dish, butter slices of bread, cut into fingers, cutting off crust, and lay over top of apple, completely covering it; sprinkle over a little sugar and bake till a delicate brown, eat with cream.

MRS. C. H. OLIPHANT

POMPADOUR PUDDING

Put 1 qt. of milk in a double boiler, bring to a boiling point. To the yolks of 3 eggs, well beaten, add ¾ cup sugar and 4 tablespoons flour, add this to the milk and cook until it thickens then remove from fire and flavor with Baker's vanilla.

FROSTING: For pudding, 3 egg whites, beaten stiff, 3 tablespoons cocoa, ½ cup sugar, spread on pudding and put in oven long enough to set the frosting.

MRS. MORRISON, MRS. SWAIN

RICE PUDDING ICED

Into 3 cups of purest drink let 1 teacup of pure rice sink and boil till all the water is gone, no matter where, stir with a with a spoon till it is smooth and white and done, then add 2 egg yolks beaten light, one lemmon rind, all grated right, and of white supar, well refined, 8 spoons by stirring, thus combine and pour the mixture into a dish of any size the cook may wish, and let it stand a while. With a fork you beat the whites as lightly as cork, the whites of those two eggs, I mean. And when they are beaten stiffly and clean, add 4 spoons of sugar white. In short, a frothing you must make, like that you put on wedding cake. Put the sweet frosting over all your pudding like a cover. In a cool oven let it brown, we think the pudding will go down.

MRS. WALLACE WHITE

RECIPES

CRANBERRY PUDDING
1 egg, 1 cup each sugar, milk and cranberries, 3 tablespoons melted butter, 2 cups flour, 2 teaspoons cream tartar, 1 teaspoon soda, bake ¾ hour, serve with sweet sauce.
MRS. FRANK M. DOUGLAS

CHOCOLATE PUDDING
1 qt. milk, 4 tablespoons cornstarch, 1 teaspoon salt, 2 squares Baker's chocolate, Baker's vanilla.
MRS. C. BRACKETT

PINEAPPLE BAVARIAN CREAM
½ box gelatine or 2 tablespoons granulated gelatine, ½ cup cold water, 1 generous cup grated pineapple, ½ cup sugar, 1 tablespoon lemon juice, whites 2 eggs, 1 bottle heavy cream, whipped. Soak gelatine in cold water, heat pineapple, add sugar, lemon juice and soaked gelatine, chill in pan of ice water, stirring constantly. **When it begins to thicken** fold in the eggs, beaten very stiffly and then the whipped cream, put in **mould** or else dish for serving, and chill.
MRS. AMY GREEN

CARAMEL CUSTARD
1 qt. milk, 5 eggs, 1 cup sugar, salt to taste. Brown sugar over fire stir constantly, taking care that it does not scorch. Pour over the browned sugar, the milk and egg mixture. Strain, and bake in pan of hot water, same as custard. Serve very cold, with whipped cream.
MRS. EVERETT H. ARCHIBALD

COFFEE SOUFFLE
Heat 1½ cups of coffee in fusion, ½ cup milk, 1 tablespoon gelatine in double boiler, ⅔ cup sugar; ⅛ teaspoon salt, yolks of 3 eggs slightly beaten. Cook until it thickens. When cold stir in the stiffly beaten whites of three eggs. Flavor with Baker's vanilla. Turn in mould. Serve plain or with whipped cream.
MRS. FREDERICK W. FOSTER

RECIPES

CHARLOTTE RUSSE
1 pint cream whipped. Stir in ⅓ box of gelatine previously dissolved in as little water as possible; 1 small cup sugar. Strain and flavor with Baker's vanilla. Line mould with lady fingers or sponge cake and fill with cream.

MRS. CARRIE E. BARNES

PINEAPPLE DELICIOUS
1 can pineapple chopped rather fine, juice of 1 lemon, juice of 1 orange, 1 lb. marshmallows, quartered. Combine and allow to stand 2 hours. Then add 1 bottle whipped cream. Serves 16 people.

MRS. W. A. GABELER

PINEAPPLE PUDDING
Scald 2¾ cups milk, mix ⅓ cup cornstarch with ¼ cup cold milk; add to the hot milk with 1 saltspoon salt and 2 tablespoons sugar. Cook 15 minutes. Add the whites 3 eggs beaten stiffly and ½ can grated pineapple. Mould, chill and serve with cream.

MRS. KIMBALL

DAY DREAM
Put 1 tablespoon of cold boiled rice into each salad dish; cover with sliced bananas, a few grapes, or any fruit you may have. Upon the top of all put a heaping mound of sweetened whipped cream.

MRS. WALLACE WHITE

ORANGE JELLY
Cover 1 box Chalmer's gelatine with 1 pt. cold water, soak 1 hour. Add 2 cups sugar and 1 pt. boiling water. Stir till dissolved. Add 1 pt. orange juice, strain and set to cool 12 hours. Other juices may be used.

MRS. HARTSHORNE

MAPLE SYRUP MOUSSE
½ cup maple syrup, ½ cup cream, yolks of 4 eggs, or 2 whole eggs, put syrup on stove, when hot stir in yolks of eggs until cooked, cool, whip cream very stiffly, mix all together, pack in ice, but do **not** churn,

MISS F. E. DODGE

RECIPES

Pies

"We live merely on the crust."   —Fronde

PIE CRUST

2½ cups pastry flour, 1 teaspoon salt, 1 teaspoon Royal baking powder, sift this 3 times, then add 1 cup lard thoroughly mixed in, and cold water; do not make it too soft.

MRS. FRANK DOUGLAS

LEMON PIE

Scald ½ cup water, 1 cup milk, ¼ cup sugar together. Add juice and rind of 1 lemon, yolks 2 eggs, ½ cup sugar, 3½ tablespoons cornstarch, little salt. Cook until thick. Cool and put into baked crust. Use whites of eggs for meringue.

MRS. ALFRED GAUNT

BANBURY TARTS

1 cup raisins, 1 cup sugar, 1 egg, 1 lemon. Grate the rind from the lemon, peel and reject the white and seeds. Put lemon and raisins through the food chopper, add other ingredients and bake in turnovers.

MRS. NEVINS

BUTTERSCOTCH PIE

1 tablespoon butter, 2 tablespoons sugar, brown together. Add yolks of 2 eggs beaten with ½ cup sugar and one tablespoon of flour. Cook in double boiler with 1½ cups hot milk until thick. When cool flavor with vanilla. Put in pastry shells and add egg whites beaten with 2 tablespoons powdered sugar.

MRS. NEVINS

BUTTERSCOTCH PIE

Yolks 3 eggs, 1½ cups brown sugar, 1 tablespoon flour, good sized piece of butter, 1 teaspoon salt, vanilla. Heat 2 cups milk. Bake in 1 crust, cover with meringue made with egg whites.

MRS. THOMPSON

RECIPES

SUMMER MINCE PIE

1 cup sugar, 2 eggs, 1 cup very sour milk, 1 cup chopped raisins, 1 tablespoon butter, ¼ teaspoon clove, ¼ teaspoon cassia, ¼ teaspoon nutmeg. Bake in a large pie or 2 small ones, with 2 crusts, beat sour milk until like a cream before adding.

MRS. WARREN HUTCHINS

PEACH PIE

Remove skins from peaches. This may be easily done after allowing peaches to stand in boiling water one minute. Cut in eighths, cook until soft with enough water to prevent burning; sweeten to taste. Cool and fill crust previously baked. Cover with whipped cream, sweetened and flavored.

MRS. WILLIAM ENOS

LEMON PIE

Rind and juice of 1 lemon, 1 cup sugar, 3 egg yolks, 1 cup milk, ½ cup water, to this add 1½ tablespoons cornstarch. Bake in 1 crust. Beat white of eggs, add ½ cup sugar, put on pie and return to oven and brown. This is delicious.

MRS. M. JAMIESON

PRUNE WHIP PIE

Soak 1 lb. of prunes over night and simmer until soft. Remove stones, cut in pieces and add: ¾ cup sugar, ¾ cup chopped walnuts. Fold in 2 egg whites beaten stiffly. Pour into baked pie shell and bake 20 minutes. When cool decorate with 1 cup whipped cream to which has been added 2 tablespoons of powdered sugar and ½ teaspoon vanilla.

MRS. CLARENCE B. SPENCE

LEMON SPONGE PIE

1 cup sugar, yolks of 2 eggs, 1 cup of milk, 1 tablespoon flour, pinch of salt, juice and rind of 1 large lemon, whites of 2 eggs beaten stiffly and added last. Bake in a slow oven. Do not open the oven door for the first 20 minutes.

MRS. JOHN OSTLER

RECIPES

MINCE MEAT

4 lbs. meat, 2 lbs. suet, 5 lbs. raisins, 2 lbs. currants, ½ lb. citron, 2 cups brown sugar, 1 quart boiled cider, 1 glass currant jelly, 1 lemon, juice and rind. 1 tablespoon allspice, 1 of cloves, 2 of cinnamon, 1 cup molasses, ½ nutmeg. Chop all and add 6 to 8 lbs. chopped apples, and 1 tablespoon salt. Cook ½ hour.

MRS. WALTER HASTINGS

MINCE MEAT

2 Bowls chopped meat, 1 bowl suet, 4 bowls apples, 2 lbs. raisins, 2 bowls molasses, 1½ bowls brown sugar, 2 dessert-spoons cinnamon, 1 dessert-spoon clove, 2 dessert-spoons salt, 1 dessert spoon allspice, 1 dessert spoon ginger, 1 dessert spoon nutmeg, 1 teaspoon black pepper, 2 cups vinegar or cider, 1 lemon.

MRS. GEORGE TENNEY

GREEN TOMATO PIE MIXTURE

Four quarts green tomatoes chopped fine, drain, cover with cold water, simmer 30 minutes and drain again. Add 2 lbs. brown sugar, 2 lbs. raisins, ½ lb. citron chopped fine, 1 tablespoon salt, ½ cup vinegar, ½ cup butter. Cook this mixture until it thickens. When cold add 1 tablespoon each of cloves, cinnamon, nutmeg. Put in jars cold and seal. Makes a good substitute for mince meat and will keep a long time.

MRS. A. H. WAGLAND, MRS.W. A. GABELER

MOCK MINCE PIE

1 lemon, ½ cup raisins, ½ cup molasses, 1 cup sugar, 1 cup boiling water, 1½ crackers rolled, ½ teaspoon cloves, 1 teaspoon cinnamon, butter size of walnut. Scald, and when cool add 1 egg.

MRS. P. C. COOK

RAISIN PIE

1 cup raisins chopped, 2 cups water, 1 cup sugar, 1 egg, tablespoon flour, juice and rind of one lemon. Mix flour, sugar, then add raisins, egg, and pour on boiling water. Boil 10 minutes. Cool. Bake in 2 crusts.

MRS. A. B. DAVIS

RECIPES

APPLE AND DATE PIE

Line deep plate with rich pastry, put in layer of sliced, tart apples, add one of cut dates and repeat until plate is full, sprinkle with cinnamon and ⅔ cup of sugar, dot with butter, put on top crust and bake in good oven.

S. B. CARROW

CHOCOLATE PIE

Stir into 1 pt. milk 3 tablespoons Baker's chocolate; when hot add ¾ cup sugar, yolks of 2 eggs, 1 tablespoon butter, 1 tablespoon cornstarch. Cook until thick and add 1 teaspoon Baker's vanilla, pour into crust same as for a custard pie, use the whites for frosting, and 3 spoons of sugar.

MRS. SUSIE J. MANN

SQUASH PIE

1 cup sifted, dry squash, 1 cup boiling milk, ⅔ cup sugar, 1 scant spoon salt, 1 teaspoon cinnamon, 2 eggs, mix in order given. This is for 1 pie.

MOCK CHERRY PIE

1 cup cranberries cut in two, ½ cup raisins, cut fine, ¾ cup sugar, 1 tablespoon flour, 1 teaspoon Baker's vanilla, mix all together in bowl, then pour in ½ cup boiling water and mix. Makes 1 pie.

MRS. A. B. DAVIS

CHEESE STRAWS

1 cup prepared (Reliable) flour, 1 cup grated cheese, 1 tablespoon butter. Rub well together and add cold water to make dough. Roll thin and cut in strips. Sprinkle pans with cold water, bake strips till golden brown. If plain flour is used put in more butter and a little salt.

MISS MORSE

RECIPES

Cakes

"Taste of sweetness, whereof a little more than a little, is much too much."   —*King Henry IV.*

MARSHMALLOW CAKE

1 cup sugar, ½ cup butter, 2 eggs, ½ cup milk 1¾ cups flour, 1 teaspoon Royal baking powder. Make cake in usual way and bake in layer tins. Filling: Place in the oven 1 half lb. marshmallows, being careful not to brown them. When melted, add to a boiled frosting made by boiling together 1 cup sugar and four tablespoons water until it threads. Add the stiffly beaten white of 1 egg, flavor with Baker's vanilla and beat until stiff enough to spread.

MRS. C. H. OLIPHANT

SILVER CAKE

1 cup of sugar, ½ cup of butter, the whites of 3 eggs, ½ cup cornstarch dissolved in nearly ½ cup of milk, 1¼ cups flour, ½ teaspoon cream of tartar, ¼ teaspoon of soda, and Baker's vanilla or almond flavor. Beat the butter to a cream and gradually beat in the sugar. Add the flavor. Mix flour, cream of tartar and soda together and sift. Beat the whites to a stiff froth. Add the cornstarch and milk to the beaten sugar and butter, then add the whites of the eggs and the flour. Mix quickly and thoroughly. Bake in a moderate oven.

MRS. W. K. EPHLIN

GOLD CAKE

One cup sugar, ½ cup butter, the yolks of 3 eggs, and 1 whole egg, ½ cup of milk; ¼ teaspoon each of soda and cream of tartar, 1¾ cups of flour. Mix the butter and sugar together and add the eggs, milk, flavor, flour in the same order named.

MRS. W. K. EPHLIN

SATIN CAKE

Yolks of 2 eggs, 1 cup sugar, scant ½ cup butter (put on back of range to soften,) 1 teaspoon cream of tartar. Stir the above to a cream, then add ½ cup sweet milk, ½ teaspoon soda dissolved in the milk, ¼ cup cornstarch sifted twice, and 1 cup pastry flour. Last of all add stiffly beaten whites of 2 eggs. Bake in pan 10x6.   MRS. FREDERICK D. HAYWARD

RECIPES

LADY CAKE

1½ cups sugar and ½ cup butter creamed together, ½ teaspoon soda in ⅔ cup milk, whites of four eggs, 1 teaspoon cream of tartar, 2 cups flour. Flavor with Baker's almond.

MISS F. E. DODGE

LAYER CAKE

½ cup butter, 1 cup sugar, ¼ cup milk, whites of 4 eggs, 1½ cups flour, ½ teaspoon cream tartar, ¼ soda. Bake in two sheets in a moderate oven. FILLING: 1 cup powdered sugar, ¼ cup hot water, simmer; add beaten white of 1 egg; when cold add ½ cup chopped raisins, ½ cup walnuts, 1 tablespoon grated cocoanut, Baker's vanilla. FROSTING: 1 cup powdered sugar to the beaten white of 1 egg. Mark frosting in squares or diamonds, place ½ walnut on each.

MRS. H. E. WOODBURY

DATE CAKE

½ cup butter, 1 cup sugar, cream together; add 1 egg beaten, 1 teaspoon soda in 1 cup sour milk, 1 teaspoon cloves, 2 cups pastry flour, 1 lb. dates chopped. Add last of all ¼ cup more sour milk (no soda.) Cook in slow oven about 45 minutes.

MRS. J. A. EMERSON

"DELICIOUS CAKE"

Cream 1 cup butter with 2 cups sugar, add beaten yolks of 3 eggs. Sift with 3 cups pastry flour, 2 teaspoons Royal baking powder; mix with above, fold in whites of eggs, well beaten. Flavor with Baker's vanilla or almond.

MRS. A. C. CROWELL

SNOW CAKE

¼ cup butter, 1 cup sugar, 2 egg whites, ½ cup milk, 1⅔ cups flour, 1½ level teaspoons Royal baking powder, ½ teaspoon Baker's vanilla.

MRS. S. C. HEAD

RECIPES

HOT MILK SPONGE CAKE

2 eggs, beaten very light, 1 cup sugar, ½ cup hot milk in which a piece of butter has been dissolved; 1 cup flour (rounding) 1 teaspoon baking powder, salt and flavoring.

MAUDE A. IRISH

HARRISON CAKE

½ cup butter, 1 cup sugar, ½ cup molasses, 2 eggs, 1 teaspoon soda, ½ cup milk, ½ teaspoon nutmeg, 1 teaspoon cinnamon, 1 teaspoon cloves, pinch of ginger, 1 cup raisins and nuts together, about 2½ cups flour.

MRS. WILLIAM ENOS

APPLE SAUCE CAKE

1 ½ cups brown sugar, ½ cup butter, 2 cups applesauce, 2½ cups flour, 1 egg, 2 teaspoons soda dissolved in applesauce, ½ cup raisins. Mix like ordinary cake.

MRS. CHARLES E. RUSSELL

DARK CHOCOLATE CAKE

1 cup sugar, 1 tablespoon butter, 1 cup sour milk, ¼ teaspoon salt, ½ cup cocoa, 1½ cups flour, 1 teaspoon soda. Mix cocoa and flour and soda together.

MRS. CHARLES E. RUSSELL

CHOCOLATE CAKE

1½ cups sugar and ½ cup butter creamed thoroughly, 2 eggs, 1 cup milk, 2 squares melted chocolate, 2 teaspoons cream of tartar, 1 teaspoon soda, 2 cups pastry flour.

FROSTING

Melt in bowl butter size of an English walnut. Mix with two squares melted chocolate and a little top milk or cream. Add confectioner's sugar little by little until right consistency. Flavor with vanilla. This is a soft frosting and very delicious.

ADELAIDE S. KAY

SUNSHINE CAKE

Beat whites 7 eggs and pinch of salt dry. Add beaten yolks 5 eggs. 1 cup sugar. Fold in 1 cup flour, ¼ teaspoon cream of tartar, in flour. 1 teaspoon vanilla. Bake 45 to 50 minutes.

MRS. FREDERICK D, HAYWARD

RECIPES

BIRTHDAY CAKE

Cream 2 oz. butter and 2 oz. sugar together. Then add 2 eggs well beaten. Next add 2 oz. currants, 1 oz. ground almonds 2¼ oz. flour, 1 teaspoon baking powder and a little flavoring Also add ½ oz. candied lemon peel and 1 oz. cherries cut in small pieces. Place in a well greased pan and bake about 1 hr.

MRS. JAGER

SPICE CAKE

1 cup sugar, ½ cup butter or lard, 1 egg, 1 cup sour milk, 1 cup raisins, 1 teaspoon soda stirred in milk, 3 tablespoons molasses, 1 teaspoon cinnamon, ½ teaspoon clove, little nutmeg, pinch of salt, 2 cups flour.

MRS. CYRUS STOWELL

DEVIL'S FOOD CAKE

½ cup butter, 2 cups sugar, 4 egg yolks, 1 cup milk, 2 cups flour, 4 teaspoons baking powder, 4 egg whites, 2 squares chocolate, ½ teaspoon vanilla. Cream the butter, add gradually ½ the sugar. Beat yolks until thick and add remaining sugar. Combine and add alternately milk and flour mixed with baking powder. Add whites of eggs beaten stiff, chocolate melted and vanilla. Bake 40 to 50 minutes. Cover with White Mountain cream or chocolate frosting.

MRS. LEVERETT PUTNAM

CREAM SPONGE CAKE

Yolks 4 eggs, 1 cup sugar, 1½ tablespoons cornstarch, 3 tablespoons cold water, flour, 1¼ teaspoons baking powder, ¼ teaspoon salt, whites 4 eggs, 1 teaspoon flavoring. Beat yolks and water until thick. Add sugar gradually; beat 2 minutes. Put cornstarch into cup and fill with flour. Sift flour, cornstarch baking powder and salt add to first mixture. When thoroughly mixed add whites beaten stiff; add flavoring. Bake in moderate oven 30 minutes in layer tins. FILLING: 1 jar cream, 1 cup sugar, 2 tablespoons cocoa, flavoring. Stir and let stand a while then whip.

MRS. WILLIAM ENOS

RECIPES

BOSTON FAVORITE CAKE

⅔ cup butter, 2 cups sugar, 4 eggs, 1 cup milk, 3½ cups flour, 5 teaspoons baking powder. This makes 2 loaves or ½ the mixture may be baked in individual tins.

MRS. LEVERETT PUTNAM

WALNUT CAKE

½ cup butter, 1 cup sugar, yolks 2 eggs, 2 whites well beaten, ½ cup milk, 1½ cups flour, 1½ teaspoons baking powder, ½ cup broken nutmeats. Bake ¾ of an hour.

MRS. C. F. KENDALL

FUDGE CAKE

1 egg, ½ small cup butter, creamed, 2 squares chocolate melted, salt and vanilla, 1⅔ cups flour with 3 level teaspoons baking powder.

MRS. PERCY HOOK

CHOCOLATE CAKE

Sift together several times 1 cup flour, 1 cup sugar, 1 teaspoon saleratus, pinch salt. Drop 2 egg yolks in hole made in mixture, 3 tablespoons butter melted in pan for cake, 1 cup sour milk, ½ cup cocoa with a little sour milk or hot water.

MRS. WM. PAISLEY

SPONGE CAKE

1 cup sifted white sugar, 1 cup flour, measured before sifting, 5 eggs. Stir the yolks and sugar together until perfectly light. Add a pinch of salt, and 1 teaspoon baking powder. Beat whites very stiff and add alternately with the flour. Flavor with 1 teaspoon lemon. Bake in slow oven (325°F) about 40 minutes.

FLORENCE E. DODGE

ANGEL CAKE

7 eggs or 8 eggs if small beaten stiff with teaspoon cream of tartar. Beat in 1 cup sugar. Fold in ⅔ cup bread flour. 1 teaspoon vanilla. Bake in tube pan about 45 minutes.

MRS. BURTON LIBBY

RECIPES

BLUEBERRY CAKE

1 cup sugar, 1 tablespoon butter, 1 egg, 3 teaspoons Royal baking powder, 1 cup milk, 1 cup blueberries, flour to make not too stiff a batter.

MRS. EVERETT ARCHIBALD

ORANGE CAKE (Fruit Frosting)

1 cup sugar, ½ cup butter, 2 eggs, 1½ cups flour, ½ cup milk, 1 teaspoon cream of tartar, ½ teaspoon soda, sift cream tartar and soda in the flour, cream butter and sugar and add the well beaten eggs, then the milk. Add the flour lightly and flavor with the grated rind of 1 orange; bake in a shallow tin.

FROSTING: ½ cup raisins, ½ cup citron, ½ cup English walnuts; break the nuts small and chop raisins and citron, white of 1 egg, 1 tablespoon lemon juice and a little of the grated orange peel, 1 teaspoon butter, melted, add confectioner's sugar until thick as required to spread, frost while cake is warm.

MRS. SKINNER

ORANGE CAKE

1½ cups sugar, ½ cup butter, ½ cup milk, 2 cups flour, 3 eggs, juice 1 orange, 1 teaspoon Royal baking powder, bake in jelly tins. Spread between layers and on top frosting made of 1 cup confectioner's sugar, white of 1 egg, rind of 1 orange, beat the white first, stirring in sugar gradually.

MRS. C. H. OLIPHANT

NUT CAKE

1 cup sugar, ½ cup butter, 2 eggs, ½ cup milk, 1½ cups flour, 2 teaspoons Royal baking powder, 1 cup nut meats.

MRS. HENRY HALL

RAISIN CAKE

2 eggs, 1 cup sugar, ½ cup butter, 1 cup raisins, ½ cup milk, 1 teaspoon cream tartar, ½ teaspoon soda, not quite ½ teaspoon all kinds of spices, a little salt, 2 cups flour.

MRS. WARREN HUTCHINS

RECIPES

BLUEBERRY CAKE

1 cup sugar, 1 tablespoon butter, 1 egg, 3 teaspoons Royal baking powder, 1 cup milk, 1 cup blueberries, flour to make not too stiff a batter.

MRS. EVERETT ARCHIBALD

ORANGE CAKE (Fruit Frosting)

1 cup sugar, ½ cup butter, 2 eggs, 1½ cups flour, ½ cup milk, 1 teaspoon cream of tartar, ½ teaspoon soda, sift cream tartar and soda in the flour, cream butter and sugar and add the well beaten eggs, then the milk. Add the flour lightly and flavor with the grated rind of 1 orange; bake in a shallow tin.
FROSTING: ½ cup raisins, ½ cup citron, ½ cup English walnuts; break the nuts small and chop raisins and citron, white of 1 egg, 1 tablespoon lemon juice and a little of the grated orange peel, 1 teaspoon butter, melted, add confectioner's sugar until thick as required to spread, frost while cake is warm.

MRS. SKINNER

ORANGE CAKE

1½ cups sugar, ½ cup butter, ½ cup milk, 2 cups flour, 3 eggs, juice 1 orange, 1 teaspoon Royal baking powder, bake in jelly tins. Spread between layers and on top frosting made of 1 cup confectioner's sugar, white of 1 egg, rind of 1 orange, beat the white first, stirring in sugar gradually.

MRS. C. H. OLIPHANT

NUT CAKE

1 cup sugar, ½ cup butter, 2 eggs, ½ cup milk, 1½ cups flour, 2 teaspoons Royal baking powder, 1 cup nut meats.

MRS. HENRY HALL

RAISIN CAKE

2 eggs, 1 cup sugar, ½ cup butter, 1 cup raisins, ½ cup milk, 1 teaspoon cream tartar, ½ teaspoon soda, not quite ½ teaspoon all kinds of spices, a little salt, 2 cups flour.

MRS. WARREN HUTCHINS

RECIPES

LIGHTNING CAKE

1 cup flour 1 cup sugar, 1 teaspoon salt, 2 teaspoons Royal baking powder, sifted together; ½ cup melted butter, 2 eggs dropped in cup, fill cup with milk, flavor with 1 teaspoon Bakers banana extract. Beat thoroughly.

MRS. C. E. RUSSELL

By adding 2 squares of melted chocolate and ½ teaspoon Baker's vanilla it makes a good chocolate cake; 1 cup raisins and ½ cup nuts, a fruit cake; divided and baked in two tins a layer cake.

MISS MAUDE FERNALD

ANGEL CAKE

1 cup unsifted flour, mixed with 1 teaspoon cream tartar, and sift 4 times. Beat whites of 10 eggs stiff. Add 1½ cups granulated sugar, beat again, salt, flavor with Baker's almond Grease and flour pan and bake 40 minutes. FROSTING: 1 cup powdered sugar, butter size of walnut, 1 teaspoon Baker's vanilla, and a little milk.

MRS. G. F. S. WEBSTER

CREAM SPONGE CAKE

Yolks of 4 eggs, 1 cup sugar, 3 tablespoons cold water, 1½ tablespoons corn starch-flour, 1½ teaspoons Royal baking powder, ¼ teaspoon salt. Whites of 4 eggs, 1 teaspoon Baker's lemon. Beat yolks of eggs until thick and lemon colored, add sugar gradually, beat two minutes, then add water. Put cornstarch in a cup, then fill with flour, add baking powder and salt, and add to first mixture, when thoroughly mixed add whites of eggs, beaten until stiff, and flavoring. Bake ½ hour in a moderate oven.

MRS. EVERETT ARCHIBALD, MRS. MIKALSON

SPONGE CAKE

3 eggs well beaten, 1 cup sugar, ⅓ cup cold water, 1 teaspoon lemon extract, salt, 1 cup flour with 1 teaspoon Royal baking powder sifted together; add whites well beaten last.

MISS L. J. MACDONALD

RECIPES

CAKE THAT NEVER FAILS

Take a cup of sugar, ¼ cup butter and cream together. Next take 2 eggs; put 1 white out for frosting and beat the rest very light and add to the creamed sugar. Next put in 2 cups flour and beat well before you add one cup milk. Beat this mixture for some time, then add 2 teaspoons Royal baking powder and one of Baker's essence of lemon.

FROSTING: The white of 1 egg peaten light, add 1 scant cup pulverized sugar, add a few drops of pink coloring. Spread over cake and shake cocoanut on the pink frosting.

MRS. WALLACE WHITE

CHOCOLATE CAKE

1 egg (yolk) 1 tablespoon sugar, ½ cup milk, 3 squares chocolate. Melt these four together till thick. Put in just before the flour, at last, ½ cup butter, 1 cup sugar, 1 whole egg and white of the other one, ½ cup milk (sweet milk) with 1 teaspoon soda dissolved in it, 2 cups pastry flour (measured after sifting) 1 teaspoon (big) Baker's vanilla. (No cream of tartar in this rule.)

MAUDE A. BUSWELL
MRS. JOHN OSTLER, MRS. WARREN HUTCHINS

MOCHA CAKE

1 large tablespoon butter and 1 cup sugar, creamed; yolk of 1 egg, ¾ cup milk, ¼ teaspoon Baker's vanilla, add 1 cup flour, sifted with 1 rounded teaspoon Royal baking powder, add 2 squares chocolate, melted. Last add beaten whites, bake in 2 layers. FILLING: Beat 1 cup powdered sugar, 1 tablespoon butter, Baker's vanilla, 2 teaspoons cocoa and 2 tablespoons coffee.

MRS. WALTER HASTINGS

SOFT CHOCOLATE FROSTING

½ cup sugar, 1½ squares chocolate, 1 tablespoon butter, ¾ cup hot water, boil slowly for 20 minutes, then add 1 tablespoon corn starch in ½ cup hot water, 1 teaspoon Baker's vanilla.

MRS. ELLIOT P. SPOONER

RECIPES

MAPLE FROSTING

1 cup Maple syrup, 1 teaspoon vinegar. Boil together until it forms a soft ball in cold water. Pour this over the beaten white of 1 egg, stir until cold, then spread.

MRS. STEPHEN E. SMITH

FILLING FOR LAYER CAKE

1 cup sugar with enough water to dissolve, let boil until it will harden in cold water. Pour slowly onto the stiffly beaten white of 1 egg, add 1 cup chopped raisins, spread on cake while warm.

MRS. WARREN HUTCHINS

Cookies

"Infinite riches in a little room."   —*Marlowe*

CHOCOLATE COOKIES

Cream ½ cup butter and 1 tablespoon lard, add 1 cup sugar then add ¼ teaspoon salt, and 2 oz. chocolate melted. Add 1 beaten egg, and ½ teaspoon soda, dissolved in 2 tablespoons milk, stir in about 2½ cups of flour. Roll thin and bake in quick oven.

MRS. JOSEPH A. BAILEY

ROCKS

1½ cups brown sugar, 1 cup butter, 2 tablespoons molasses, 1 cup chopped raisins, 1 cup broken walnuts, 3 eggs, a pinch of salt, 1 teaspoon soda in 2½ cups flour. Mix in the order given and drop from a teaspoon ½ inch apart on a greased and floured tin.

MRS. HUGH SMITH

ROXBURY CAKES

½ cup butter, ½ cup sugar, yolks of 2 eggs, ½ cup molasses, ½ cup sour milk, 1½ cups flour, ½ cup raisins; ½ cup nuts, 1 teaspoon cinnamon, ½ teaspoon clove, a little nutmeg; 1 teaspoon soda, whites of 2 eggs (beaten stiff.) Bake in little tins and frost with white frosting.

MRS. ALFRED GAUNT

RICE FLAKE MACAROONS

1 tablespoon butter, 1 cup sugar, 2 eggs, 4 cups flakes and 1 teaspoon Royal baking powder. Flavor to taste.

MRS. D. D. WOODBURY

RECIPES

PRAIRIE NUGGETS

1 cup butter, 1½ cups brown sugar, 3 eggs beaten together until thick, 1 level teaspoon soda, 3 cups flour, ½ teaspoon salt, ½ teaspoon each of cinnamon, cloves, allspice, nutmeg, a few grains of white pepper, ¼ cup hot water, 1½ cups raisins cut small, ⅓ cup currants, 1 cup citron, lemon, and orange peel, use a little less of citron than peel, 1 cup English walnuts broken not very finely. To put together: Cream the butter, add sugar gradually, then the well beaten eggs, add the soda dissolved in the ¼ cup hot water. Sift flour, spices and all dry ingredients together, then divide it between the nuts and fruit and add to cake. Drop by half teaspoon on buttered tins, an inch apart. Bake in moderate oven. All measures are level.

MRS. MIKALSON

ONE-EGG CAKES

1 cup sugar, ½ cup butter, 1 egg, 1 cup milk, 2½ cups flour (sifted pastry) 2 heaping teaspoons Royal baking powder sifted 3 times with the flour. Bake in gem pans. Will make 2 dozen.

MRS. GEORGE TENNEY

DATE AND NUT BAR

1 cup brown sugar, 1 cup flour, ½ teaspoon baking powder, ¼ teaspoon salt, 1 cup chopped dates, 1 cup chopped nuts, butter size of walnut, 2 eggs. Cream butter and sugar, add beaten eggs and then dry ingredients and lastly fruit and nuts. Bake in square tin in moderate oven 15 minutes.

MRS. WILLIAM ENOS

MOLASSES COOKIES

1 cup sugar, 2 eggs (beaten) ½ cup molasses ⅔ cup half butter and half lard, 1 teaspoon soda, 1 teaspoon cinnamon, ½ teaspoon clove, ¼ teaspoon mace, 3 teaspoons flour, or enough to roll.

MRS. E. JENKINSON

BROWNIES

2 eggs beaten, 1 cup sugar, ⅓ cup butter melted with 2 squares chocolate, ¾ cup flour, teaspoon baking powder, ⅓ cup milk, 1 cup chopped nuts. vanilla.

MRS. C. F. KENDALL

RECIPES

HERMIT COOKIES

½ cup sugar, ⅔ cup shortening (⅓ lard), creamed together; 1 egg, ½ cup molasses with 1 dessert sp. soda, 1 tablespoon vinegar, 2 tablespoons water, ½ teaspoon salt, ½ teaspoon cinnamon, ½ teaspoon cloves, ¼ teaspoon ginger. Sift 3 cups pastry flour. 1 cup cut and floured raisins. Roll, not too thin, and cut. Hot oven— 450° F.

FLORENCE E. DODGE

GINGER SNAPS

Bring to a boil 1 cup molasses, stir in 1 dessert spoon soda, pour it while foaming over 1 cup of sugar, 1 tablespoon ginger, 1 of vinegar beaten together, flour enough to roll. Stir as lightly as possible.

MRS. HOOK

ICE BOX COOKIES

1 cup butter, 2 cups light brown sugar, 2 eggs, 1 level teaspoon baking powder, ½ teaspoon salt, 1 cup chopped nuts, 3½ cups flour. Cream butter and sugar, add eggs, sift flour, baking powder and salt twice, and add to first mixture with nuts. Pack in bread tin, set in refrigerator over night, turn out on bread board, slice very thin and bake in hot oven.

MRS. C. F. KENDALL

WAFFLES

Mix and sift 2 cups flour, 3 teaspoons baking powder, 1 teaspoon salt, 1 tablespoon sugar; add yolks 3 eggs beaten, 1½ cups milk, 3 tablespoons shortening melted. Fold in whites of 3 eggs beaten.

MRS. BAKETEL

OATMEAL COOKIES

1 egg, 1 cup sugar, 1 cup melted lard and butter, 1 tablespoon molasses, 4 tablespoons sweet milk, 1 teaspoon soda, 1 teaspoon cinnamon, 2½ cups rolled oats, 2½ cups sifted flour. Roll thin and bake in a moderately hot oven.

RUTH NORRIS

RECIPES

FILLED COOKIES

1 egg, 1 cup sugar, ½ cup shortening, ½ cup milk, 1 teaspoon soda, 2 teaspoons cream tartar, 3½ cups flour.
FILLING: Cook together being careful not to burn, 1 cup chopped raisins, ½ cup sugar, ½ cup water, 1 teaspoon flour, flavor lemon juice. Cut out a cookie, place a little filling on it, lay another cookie on top. Do not wet the edges of cookies. Bake in moderate oven.

      MRS. A. E. HEALD, MRS. MORRISON
         MRS. ALFRED GAUNT

DATE CAKES

1 cup sugar, ⅔ cup butter, 1 cup dates cut fine, 1 egg, salt. Beat together and add 1 teaspoon soda, 2 teaspoons cream tartar 2 cups bread flour, ½ cup milk, ½ teaspoon cassia.

         GRACE BANNISTER
      MRS. GEORGE BLODGETT

PEANUT COOKIES

1 tablespoon butter, 2 tablespoons sugar, 2 tablespoons milk, 1 egg well beaten, ½ cup flour, ½ teaspoon Royal baking powder, ½ teaspoon salt, ½ cup finely chopped peanuts. Cream the butter, add the sugar, milk and egg. Sift together thoroughly the flour, baking powder and salt, and add to the mixture, then add the peanuts. Drop by teaspoonfuls on an unbuttered tin ½ inch apart, place ½ peanut on each and bake in slow oven.

        MRS. CHAS. KENDALL

PEANUT COOKIES

1 large tablespoon butter, ½ cup sugar, 1 egg, 2 tablespoons milk, 1 cup flour, 1 even teaspoon Royal baking powder, ½ teaspoon salt, ¾ cup chopped peanuts. Cream butter and sugar, add beaten egg and milk. Sift flour, salt and baking powder and add to other ingredients with the chopped peanuts. Drop by teaspoonfuls on buttered tins about 2 inches apart, put half a peanut on top of each and bake in a quick oven.

        MRS. HARRY H. JOHNSON

RECIPES

NUT WAFERS

1 cup brown sugar, 1 tablespoon molasses, 2 eggs, ½ cup flour, ¼ teaspoon Royal baking powder, salt, 1 cup chopped and floured walnuts. Drop from a teaspoon on buttered tins. hot oven.

MRS. H. E. WOODBURY

SUGAR COOKIES

1 cup sugar, ½ cup butter creamed; add 1 beaten egg, ⅓ cup milk, 1 teaspoon Baker's vanilla, ½ teaspoon soda, 1 teaspoon cream tartar, sifted with flour to roll out, and cut thin.

MISS L. J. MACDONALD
MRS. J. A. EMERSON

CHOCOLATE HERMITS

½ cup butter, ⅔ cup sugar, 2 eggs, ½ cup raisins, seeded, ¼ teaspoon salt, 2 teaspoons Royal baking powder, 2 cups flour, ¼ cup chocolate, powdered, 2 tablespoons hot water, 1 teaspoon cinnamon. Cream butter, add sugar, eggs, raisins, flour in which baking powder has been sifted, chocolate melted in water, salt and cinnamon. Drop from teaspoon on a buttered baking sheet, put a raisin in the center of each hermit and bake in a moderate oven.

MRS. WILLIAM HIGH

HERMIT COOKIES

1 cup sugar, ½ cup butter, 1 beaten egg, 2 tablespoons sour milk, 1 cup chopped raisins, ½ teaspoon clove, nutmeg, cinnamon, ½ teaspoon soda dissolved in the sour milk. Flour to roll.

MRS. J. A. BAILEY

GINGER SNAPS

1 cup light brown sugar, ⅔ cup butter, ½ cup cold water, 1 egg, ⅔ cup molasses, 1 large tablespoon ginger, 1 large teaspoon soda. Flour to make thick batter. Drop by teaspoonfuls on a well greased pan, bake in moderate oven.

SUSANNAH FIELDHOUSE

RECIPES

GINGERBREAD
½ cup sugar, ½ cup shortening, 1 cup molasses, 1 teaspoon soda dissolved in little hot water, then fill cup with cold water, salt, ½ teaspoon cinnamon, ½ teaspoon ginger. Flour, not too thick.
F. E. DODGE

CREAM CAKE SHELLS
1 cup cold water, ½ cup butter, let come to a boil and stir in 1 heaping cup flour. When cold add 3 eggs, one at a time. Beat thoroughly. Bake in a quick oven 20 minutes.
MRS. GEORGE TENNEY

GINGERBREAD
½ cup molasses, ½ cup sugar, ½ cup butter, scant, ⅔ cup sour milk, 1 egg, ½ teaspoon ginger, 1¾ cups flour (pastry), 1 teaspoon soda. Lard may be substituted for half the butter.
MRS. HUGH SMITH

DOUGHNUTS
1 cup sugar, 2 eggs (not beaten) pinch nutmeg, and ½ teaspoon salt, 1 cup sweet milk, 4 tablespoons melted lard, 2 even teaspoons cream tartar, 1 even teaspoon soda, ½ teaspoonful Baker's vanilla, pastry flour to roll.
MISS STEVENS

SOUR MILK DOUGHNUTS
1½ cups sugar, ½ cup butter, 4 eggs, 1 cup sour milk, 1 teaspoon soda, little ginger, add flour to make them stiff to roll out and fry.
MISS HATTIE STEVENS

DOUGHNUTS
4 heaping cups **bread** flour, in which sift 2 teaspoons cream tartar and 1 of soda, 1 teaspoon salt, little nutmeg, sift 4 times, 1¼ cups sugar, 2 eggs broken in sugar, beat; 1¼ cups sweet milk, 1 iron mixing spoon sweet cream. Mix, and add more flour if needed. Make stiff enough to handle easily.
MRS. J. A. EMERSON

RECIPES

DOUGHNUTS

2 cups sugar, 2 eggs, 1½ cups milk, 2 teaspoons melted butter, 2 teaspoons cream tartar 1 teaspoon soda, a little cassia or nutmeg, salt. Flour to roll.

MRS. EVERETT H. ARCHIBALD

DOUGHNUTS

Sift 3 cups bread flour 4 times with 1 teaspoon salt, 3 level teaspoons baking powder, little nutmeg. Break 1 egg into bowl, add melted butter size of egg, ⅔ cup sugar, ¼ cup sweet cream. Add above to flour mixture and enough more to make stiff.

MRS. WILLIAM H. BUSWELL

DOUGHNUTS

1 cup of sugar, 1 teaspoon of soda, ½ teaspoon of ginger ½ teaspoon of nutmeg, ½ teaspoon of salt. Mix thoroughly; add 2 well beaten eggs, 1 cup sour milk, 4 cups bread flour and 1 teaspoon cream tartar sifted 3 times. No more flour will be needed. Stir in gradually.

MRS. D. D. WOODBURY

DOUGHNUTS

2 cups sour milk, 1 good teaspoon soda, 2 even teaspoons salt, little nutmeg, stir well. Add 1½ cups sugar, add some bread flour. Break into the mixture 1 egg; add flour enough to make as soft as you can handle. Roll and cut.

FLORENCE E. DODGE

Bread

*"A loaf of bread, the Walrus said,
is what we chiefly need."*
—Carroll

HOT ROLLS

2 cups milk scalded, ½ cup butter, 4 tablespoons sugar, 1 yeast cake, flour to make stiff, after which add, with the hands, the whites of 2 eggs beaten to a stiff froth. Rise. Roll out thin, cut in rounds, fold with butter between. Let rise again; bake.

MRS. GEORGE TENNEY

RECIPES

GRAHAM GEMS
Sift together 1 cup graham flour, 1 cup white flour, ½ teaspoon salt, 1½ heaping teaspoons cream tartar, 1 heaping teaspoon soda. Cream a piece of butter the size of an egg, and ½ cup of sugar, add 1 beaten egg and 1 cup warm milk, then stir into dry ingredients.
MRS. EVERETT H. ARCHIBALD

GRAHAM BREAD (not raised)
2 cups sour milk, ⅔ cup molasses, 1 heaping teaspoon soda ½ teaspoon salt, 1 cup flour, graham enough to make thick to drop from spoon. Put in loaf-tin and bake slowly 1½ hours. This makes 1 loaf.
MRS. MAUD A. BUSWELL

Same rule with ⅓ cup brown sugar, instead of molasses.
MRS. H. A. DODGE

ENTIRE WHEAT BREAD
2 cups scalded milk, ⅓ cup sugar or 1/3 cup molasses, 1 teaspoon salt, 1 yeast cake dissolved in ¼ cup luke warm water 4⅔ cups entire wheat flour. Add sweetening and salt to milk; cool, when luke warm, add dissolved yeast cake and flour; beat well, cover, and let rise to double its bulk. Again beat, and turn into buttered bread pans, having pans **half** full; let rise and bake. Entire wheat bread should not quite double its bulk during last rising. This mixture may be baked in gem pans.
MRS. AMY GREENE

ENTIRE WHEAT GEMS
1 cup sour milk, 1 cup entire wheat, ¼ teaspoon salt, ½ teaspoon soda, 1 egg, 1 dessertspoon sugar. Drop in gem pans and bake quickly in hot oven.
MRS. MAUDE A. BUSWELL

ENTIRE WHEAT BREAD
2 cups sour milk, ½ cup sugar, 2⅔ cups entire wheat flour, 2 teaspoons soda, ½ teaspoon salt. Bake slowly 1 hour.
MRS. D. D. WOODBURY

RECIPES

BROWN BREAD
1 cup rye, ¾ cup Indian meal, ¾ cup flour, ½ cup molasses 1 cup sour milk, ½ cup water or sweet milk, 1 teaspoon soda dissolved in water and strained. A stale doughnut dissolved into the batter improves it, or a bit of cake. It should pour into the steamer. Steam 4 hours at the least.

MRS. WALTER HASTINGS

NUT BREAD
½ cup sugar, ¾ cup milk, ⅔ teaspoon soda, ½ teaspoon salt, 1 egg well beaten, 2 cups bread flour, 1½ teaspoons cream tartar, ½ cup broken nuts. Mix together with spoon (soft like gem mixture) pour into pan and let rise 20 minutes. Bake ½ hour.

MRS. E. W. A. JENKINSON

ORANGE TEA BISCUIT
2 cups sifted flour, ¾ cup milk, 3 tablespoons butter, 2 tablespoons sugar, 4 teaspoons baking powder 1 teaspoon salt, grated rind of 1 orange. Dip 1 tablet of sugar in orange juice and press in top of biscuit before baking. Delicious served hot.

MRS. HARRISON

BROWN BREAD
½ cup corn meal, 1 cup graham flour, 1 cup white flour, ½ cup rye flour; mix together; 1 teaspoon salt, 1 teaspoon soda dissolved in water, scant cup molasses, 2 cups cold water. Steam 3 hours.

MRS. WILLIAM ENOS

COCOANUT MUFFINS
1 teaspoon butter, 2 dessertspoons sugar, 1 egg, 1 cup milk, scant 1½ cup flour, 2 teaspoons baking powder, salt, 3 teaspoons cocoanut or dates may be used. This makes 8 muffins.

MRS. ELIZABETH HOOK

BLUEBERRY OR APPLE MUFFINS
2½ cups flour, 3 rounded teaspoons baking powder, ½ cup sugar, ½ teaspoon salt, 1 egg (beaten light) ⅓ cup melted Crisco, 1 cup milk, 1 heaping cup blueberries or finely cut apple. Makes 15 muffins.

MRS. R. C. NORRIS

RECIPES

DARK GRAHAM BREAD (not raised)

2 cups butter milk, ⅔ cup molasses, 1 heaping teaspoon soda (in bowl with molasses poured over) 1 teaspoon salt, 1 cup bread flour, 2 cups entire wheat flour, ½ cup cut-up raisins (or nuts.)

MRS. WILLIAM H. BUSWELL

NUT BREAD

Mix and sift 4 cups flour, 7 teaspoons baking powder, 2 tablespoons brown sugar, 2 teaspoons salt. Add 1½ cups milk to which has been added 1 well beaten egg. Add 1 or 1½ cups broken nut meat. Bake in a buttered loaf pan about 45 minutes.

MRS. W. O. PAISLEY

WHOLE WHEAT BREAD

Dissolve a cake of yeast in a cup of lukewarm water. Mix two cups of fresh milk with a pint of scalding water, add a teaspoon salt and 1 of sugar and let stand until it too is lukewarm, then stir in the dissolved yeast. Add a quart of whole wheat flour, or enough to make a batter that can be beaten. Beat hard for five minutes, then add flour enough to make a dough that can be kneaded easily. Knead for 10 minutes and set to rise in a warm place. It should be light in about 3 hours. Knead for five minutes more, let rise in greased bread pans about 1½ hours and bake in moderate oven 50 to 60 minutes.

MRS. JAGER

GRAHAM MUFFINS

½ cup sugar, scant, 1 tablespoon shortening, cream; 1 egg, 1 tablespoon molasses, 1 teaspoon baking powder, ½ teaspoon salt, ½ teaspoon soda in 1 cup sour milk, ½ cup hot water, ½ cup bran (Pillsbury's Health) 1 cup pastry flour, 1 cup graham meal (or entire wheat) Bake in muffin pans. Makes 15 muffins.

MRS. HATTIE WARDWELL

RECIPES

GINGER BREAD

1 pint flour, 1 teaspoon soda, salt, ½ cup shortening, fill cup with boiling water, 1 cup molasses, ½ teaspoon cassia, 1 teaspoon ginger. Pour cup of water and shortening into mixing bowl, add molasses, cassia, ginger and salt, sift flour and soda 3 times and add to other ingredients.

MRS. CHARLES E. RUSSELL

OATMEAL BREAD

Pour upon 2 cups oatmeal, 1 quart boiling water, add ½ cup molasses, ½ cup sugar, 1 tablespoon salt and 1 tablespoon lard; when lukewarm add ½ yeast cake dissolved in warm water, add enough flour to make as stiff as white bread.

JANE WHITTIER

OAT MEAL GEMS

To 1 cup oat meal, soaked in 1 cup water over night, add 1 cup white flour, 2 teaspoons Royal baking powder, 2 eggs, ½ cup sweet milk, and ½ teaspoon salt.

SPONGE CORN CAKE

⅓ cup sugar, yolks of 2 eggs, white of 1 egg (1 egg would do), 1 cup sour milk, ½ teaspoon soda, ½ teaspoon salt, 1 cup flour, ½ cup corn meal.

MISS F. E. DODGE

SQUASH MUFFINS

1 cup sifted squash, 3 cups flour, ½ cup sugar, 1 teaspoon butter, 1 teaspoon soda, 2 teaspoons cream tartar, milk enough to make a stiff batter. Bake in a quick oven.

MRS. CHARLES H. MANN

RYE GEMS

1 cup rye meal, 1 cup flour, ¼ cup sugar, 1 cup milk, salt, 2 teaspoons Royal baking powder, 1 egg, 1 tablespoon butter. Sift together flour, sugar, baking powder and salt, add milk, egg and butter. Bake in gem pans.

MRS. KING

RECIPES

CORN CAKE

1 egg, 1 cup white flour, ¾ cup Indian meal, 1 teaspoon salt ¼ cup melted butter, 1 cup sweet milk or sour, ½ cup sugar, 2 teaspoons Royal baking powder with **sweet** milk or 1 teaspoon soda with sour milk.

WINNIFRED BANNISTER
MRS. CARRIE E. BARNES
MRS. A. B. DAVIS

Same Rule, ¼ cup instead of 1 cup flour.

MRS. HARRY H. JOHNSON

CREAM MUFFINS

To make 1 dozen beat up 1 egg very light, mix with 4 tablespoons rich sweet cream, a little salt and a scant ½ cup milk. Sift in slowly 1¼ cups whole wheat flour and 2 teaspoons Royal baking powder. Bake in a very quick oven 15 or 20 minutes, putting very little butter in each muffin pan that the muffins may puff up and be nearly all crust.

MRS. MIKALSON

RICE MUFFINS

2½ cups flour, 1 cup milk, 1 egg, ½ teaspoon salt, ¾ cup hot cooked rice, 5 teaspoons Royal baking powder 2 tablespoons melted butter, 2 tablespoons sugar. Mix dry ingredients, sift, add ½ milk, egg well beaten, the remainder of milk with rice and beat thoroughly, then add butter.

MRS. KING

FLOUR MUFFINS

1 egg, 2 tablespoons butter, 1½ cups pastry flour, 2½ teaspoons Royal baking powder, ½ cup sugar, salt, 1 cup milk.

MRS. C. A. CARLETON

FLUTTER DUCKS

1 egg, ¼ cup sugar, 1 cup milk, 2 cups flour, 2 teaspoons cream tartar, 1 teaspoon soda, butter size of egg, melted and added last. Bake in muffin pans.

MRS. KING

RYE MUFFINS

2 cups sour milk, 2 cups rye meal, 1 cup flour, 2/3 cup sugar 1 egg, salt, 1 teaspoon soda, little melted butter.

MRS. ROY V. BAKETEL

RECIPES

CREAM TARTAR BISCUIT
Sift 1 quart bread flour with 2 heaping teaspoons cream of tartar, 1 teaspoon soda and 1 teaspoon salt, 3 times. Mix with this 1 tablespoon lard or butter. Moisten with sweet milk. Roll to about an inch in thickness and cut with small cutter. Place a small piece of lard on each biscuit. Bake 15 minutes in a very hot oven.   MRS. FRANK M. DOUGLAS

RYE PANCAKES
1 egg, 1 tablespoon molasses, 1 cup sour milk, 2 cups rye meal (or you can use ⅓ flour and ⅔ rye) salt. Drop in smoking fat, drain on paper. Serve with maple syrup.
MRS. M. A. BUSWELL

PAN CAKES
½ cup Indian meal, ¾ cup rye flour, ¾ white flour, 1 cup sweet milk, 1 tablespoon sugar, 1 egg, 1 teaspoon cream tartar, ½ teaspoon soda, salt. Drop from spoon into deep hot fat.
MRS. G. F. S. WEBSTER

Preserves and Pickles

"Everye white will have its blacke, and everye sweet its soure" —Percy (*Peliques*)

MARMALADE
6 oranges, 3 grape fruit, 6 qts. water, cut fruit in thin slices cover with water for 24 hours, cook all together until soft, then take from stove and let stand 24 hours. Take 1 pt. of the mixture to 1 pt. of sugar, and boil until thick.
S. B. CARROW; J. W. CHAMLEY

BAKED APPLES
Pare and **core** the apples, roll in syrup made of sugar and water, or maple syrup, then roll in fine bread crumbs, add bits of butter and sugar, bake until apples are soft. After taking from the oven, fill the holes where the cores were removed with broken walnuts or hickory nuts, placing a half nut on top, serve with plain or whipped cream.
MRS. HUGH SMITH

RECIPES

CRANBERRY-APPLE SAUCE

Stew 1 qt. cranberries till soft enough to crush and strain, sweeten to taste and put liquid back to stew with 3 large apples that have been carefully peeled and sliced.

MRS. STEPHEN E. SMITH

CHILI SAUCE

12 large tomatoes, 3 onions, 3 peppers, chopped, ½ cup sugar, 1 cup vinegar, 2 teaspoons salt, 2 teaspoons cinnamon. Add the vinegar after the mixture has been cookiug, also the spice. Remove part of the seeds of the peppers.

CHILI SAUCE

24 large ripe tomatoes, 8 large onions, 2 red peppers, 2 cups brown sugar, 1 quart vinegar, 1 teaspoon each of cassia, cloves, ginger, allspice, 2 tablespoons salt. Boil together until thick.

MRS. HENRY GAUNT

FINE RULE FOR CUCUMBER PICKLES

1 cup mustard, 1 cup salt, 1 gal. vinegar, 1 pk. cucumbers. Wash cucumbers and put in crock. Pour over the gallon of vinegar, sift over all the mustard and salt. Cover and put away. These are good for 2 years.

MRS. H. A. DODGE

POTTSFIELD PICKLE

3 lbs. green tomatoes, 3 lbs. ripe tomatoes, 3 red peppers, 1 quart small onions, 2 bunches celery, 1 cabbage or 2 quarts; chop ingredients, put on ½ cup salt, let remain over night then drain, add 3 pints vinegar, 3 pints sugar, ½ cup white mustard seed, 1 teaspoon cinnamon, 1 teaspoon cloves. Cook from 10 to 30 minutes.

MRS. GEORGE TENNEY

FOREIGN FRUIT PRESERVE

1 pk. hard pears, peeled, quartered and sliced the short way. Add 1 cup cold water. Boil until quite soft, stirring as little as possible. Add 3 lbs. sugar, and a small jar of preserved ginger cut into small pieces. Simmer slowly on back of the stove 7 hours. Add 6 lemons cut in thin slices and quartered, a little before it is done.

MRS. BARKER

RECIPES

PICALILLY

1 peck green tomatoes, 1 small cabbage, 2 quarts large peppers, 2 quarts onions. Chop, mix and cover with 3 cups salt. Let stand over night. Press out every particle of water. Put in stone crock and pour in boiling hot the following pickle: 1 quart vinegar, 4 lbs. sugar, 2 tablespons mixed whole spice, 2 oz. stick cinnamon, ½ oz. whole cloves, (spices tied in a muslin bag). Add 2 cups grated horseradish and stir thoroughly.

MRS. C. H. OLIPHANT

SLICED GREEN TOMATO SWEET PICKLE

1 peck green tomatoes sliced thin, 1 dozen large onions sliced thin. Boil together with 2 qts. vinegar, 2 qts water, 1 large cup salt, until tender. Throw this liquid away, and press out all water. Add to pickle No. 1, 4 lbs. sugar, 1 qt. vinegar, 2 tablespoons each of whole or allspice and stick cinnamon, 1 tablespoon each mustard seed and cloves, 1 tablespoon ground ginger, ½ teaspoon cayenne pepper. Put in mixture and boil together ½ hour.

MRS. C. H. OLIPHANT

OR PICKLE NO. 2: Mix with 1 lb. brown sugar, 1 qt. vinegar, 1 tablespoon mustard seed, 1 tablespoon whole allspice, 1 tablespoon ground ginger, ½ teaspoon red pepper, 1 teaspoon whole cloves. Boil 5 minutes.

MISS BESSIE SWAN

PICKLE RELISH

Chop together: 12 green tomatoes, 12 apples, 4 onions, 4 peppers, 1 cup raisins. Add 1 qt. vinegar, 2 cups brown sugar, 2 tablespoons mustard seed, 2 tablespoons powdered sugar, 2 tablespoons salt, 1 tablespoon ginger. Cook 1 hour.

PEPPER RELISH

12 green peppers, 12 red peppers, 14 large onions. Cover with hot water. Stand 10 minutes; drain. Cover with hot water; stand 20 minutes; drain. Add 3 cups sugar, 1 qt. vinegar, 3 tablespoons salt. Boil 18 minutes.

MRS. W. O. PAISLEY

APPLE CHUTNEY

12 green tomatoes, 12 green apples, 4 bell peppers, 8 onions, 2 cups seedless raisins, 6 cups brown sugar, 6 cups vinegar, ¼ cup salt, 1 oz. mustard seed. Chop and simmer 1 hour.

MRS. THOMPSON

RECIPES

ENGLISH LEMON CURD

½ lb. loaf sugar, 2 eggs, ½ lb. butter, juice 3 lemons and rind of 2. Cook in double boiler until thick as honey. Can be used in sandwiches or cake.

MRS. HARRISON

TOMATO CATSUP

Scald and peel 50 tomatoes. Add 4 cups vinegar, 4 cups sugar, 4 red peppers chopped, 4 onions chopped, 4 large spoons salt. Cook 3 hours, strain and seal.

MRS. H. E. MOORE

PEPPER RELISH

1 doz. green peppers, 1 doz. red peppers, 1 doz. onions, 2 cups sugar, 1 qt. vinegar, 2 tablespoons salt. Chop all together. Cook all until tender.

MRS. FREDERICK W. FOSTER

Candy

"Linked sweetness long drawn out." —Milton

COCOA FUDGE

1½ cups milk, 6 level tablespoons cocoa, 3 level tablespoons butter, pinch salt, 2½ cups powdered sugar, 1 teaspoon Baker's vanilla, mix all ingredients but vanilla, stirring constantly until it begins to boil, then cook slowly, stirring occasionally, 8 or 10 minutes; when cooked add vanilla and pour into buttered pan.

MAUD L. HEAD

PEPPERMINTS

1 cup granulated sugar, 4 dessertspoons cold water, boil 2 minutes, add 1 cup confectioner's sugar, sifted beforehand, 4 drops oil of peppermint, drop quickly on marble or white oil cloth.

MRS. J. W. BODWELL

RECIPES

CREAM MINTS

2 cups sugar, ½ cup hot water, stir until melted, not stirring after it begins to boil, boil 8 minutes, remove from fire, add 4 drops flavor and drop on waxed paper.

MRS. S. B. CARROW

CORN FLAKE KISSES

Whites of 2 eggs beaten very stiff, 1 cup sugar, 1 cup cocoanut, 2 cups corn flakes, 1 teaspoon vanilla. Mix quickly and drop in teaspoonfuls on baking tin quite far apart. Bake in quick oven 15 or 20 minutes.

RUTH NORRIS

COCOANUT CANDY

2 cups white sugar, 1 cup grated cocoanut, 1 teaspoon Baker's almond, ½ cup milk, 2 teaspoons butter, melted in sauce pan, add milk and sugar, stir until dissolved, boil to form soft ball in cold water, not stirring. Remove from fire, beat till creamy, pour into pan, mark into bars.

MRS. S. B. CARROW

CHOCOLATE CARAMELS

3 lbs. brown sugar, ½ lb. chocolate, 1 cup milk, 1 tablespoon butter, Baker's vanilla, put materials together, boil rapidly. stirring until it forms soft ball, then beat until thick, turn into pans, mark in squares.

MRS. S. B. CARROW

BUTTER TAFFY

Piece butter size of an egg, ½ cup water, 1 cup sugar, 1 tablespoon molasses, 2 tablespoons vinegar, boil 20 minutes, pour into a buttered tin and cut into squares when cool.

MRS. KIMBALL

PENUCHE

3 cups brown sugar, 1 cup milk or cream, butter size of a walnut, 1 cup chopped walnuts. Boil sugar and milk together until a "soft ball" forms in cold water, then add the butter. Take from the fire and beat well, adding the nuts and Baker's vanilla. Pour into a buttered pan to harden.

RUTH MORRISON

RECIPES

PUFFED RICE BRITTLE
Boil 1 cup granulated sugar, ½ cup water, 1 teaspoon vinegar five minutes; add 2 teaspoons molasses, butter size of walnut, ½ teaspoon salt, boil until it is brittle in cold water; take from fire and stir in ½ package puffed rice previously warmed. Pour into pans.   MRS. SUSIE J. MANN

PUFFED RICE CANDY
Boil 1 cup molasses, 1 cup brown sugar, 2 tablespoons vinegar, butter size of walnut. Crisp 1 package puffed rice and put in buttered pan and turn the boiled mixture over it and stir.
                                            MILDRED A. FOSTER

SEA FOAM CANDY
2 cups brown sugar, ½ cup water, 1 tablespoon vinegar, 1 teaspoon Baker's vanilla, white of 1 egg, ½ cup walnuts. Boil together the sugar, water and vinegar until it threads on the spoon. Beat the egg white stiff. Gradually pour the syrup onto the egg. Add nuts and vanilla. Drop from the spoon upon oiled or waxed paper.
                                            ......F. A. RAFFERTY

DATE FUDGE
2 cups granulated sugar, ½ cup milk, butter size of a walnut, 2 squares chocolate, 1 teaspoon Baker's vanilla, ¼ lb. dates cut in pieces. Boil 4 minutes and beat until creamy. Pour into pan.
                                                S. B. CARROW

BROWN SUGAR CANDY
1 heaping cup brown sugar, ¼ cup milk. Boil until it begins to candy. Then add Baker's vanilla and chopped nutmeats. Put in greased tin. Mark in squuares.
                                                F. E. DODGE

DIVINITY FUDGE
½ cup Karo corn syrup, ½ cup boiling water, 2 cups sugar. Boil 4 minutes or until it has the consistency of chocolate fudge when that is removed from the fire. Pour it very slowly upon the beaten white of an egg, stirring briskly all the time. Add ½ teaspoon Baker's vanilla, and a cup walnut meats. Beat until stiff enough to pour into buttered pan.
                                            MRS. A. C. GAUNT

RECIPES

MOLASSES CANDY

1 cup sugar and ½ cup water; boil 3 minutes, then add 1 cup molasses, butter size of walnut and a pinch of soda. Cook until hard, but not brittle when dropped in water. Pour into buttered pan and pull as soon as cool.

MRS. SMITH

Miscellaneous

CHOCOLATE

Put 2 or 3 squares of chocolate, sugar and a quart of milk a double boiler. Cook for ½ hour and then beat vigorously with a Dover egg beater. Flavor with Baker's vanilla. If desired particulaly rich and nourishing, pour boiling over 1 or 2 beaten eggs. In serving place 1 marshmallow in each cup.

DR. AGNES FRASER

FRUIT PUNCH

Juice of 1 dozen lemons, ½ dozen oranges, 1 jar of pineapple, 1 jar raspberries, sweeten to taste.

MRS. W. A. GABELER

CORN MEAL GRUEL

2 teaspoons corn meal, ¼ teaspoon salt, ½ cup milk, 2 cups boiling water. Mix corn meal, salt and milk, add boiling water and cook in double boiler 2 hours.

MRS. C. E. RUSSELL

OLD FASHIONED SPRUCE BEER

9 quarts water, 1 yeast cake, 4 cups sugar, 8 drops oil of spruce, 16 drops oil of wintergreen, 24 drops oil of sassafras. Put in beer bottles and cover, it will be ready to use in 24 hours.

CARRIE E. BARNES
MRS. J. A. EMERSON

TWO SUMMER DRINKS

(1) Equal parts grape juice and strong lemonade sweetened to taste and served with chopped ice.   (2) Equal parts grape juice and ginger ale served with chopped ice.

DR. AGNES FRASER

RECIPES

SHREDDED WHEAT BISCUIT (for Breakfast)
Warm the biscuit in the oven to restore crispness, don't burn; pour hot milk over it, dipping the milk over it until the shreds are swollen, then pour a little cream over the top of the biscuit, or serve with cold milk or cream, according to individual taste.

SAUCE
Beat together white 1 egg, ½ cup sugar. Add beaten yolk ½ cup whipped cream, flavor.
MRS. JENKINSON

HOT CHOCOLATE SAUCE
4 squares chocolate, 2 cups sugar, 1 cup thin cream, butter size of egg, vanilla. Boil all 10 minutes and serve.
MRS. WILLIAM BUSWELL

JAM—QUINCE, APPLE AND PUMPKIN
1 qt. chopped quince, 1 pint chopped apple, 1 pt. chopped pumpkin, 2 lbs. sugar, 1 pint water. Mix all together, cook until soft.
MRS. WILLIAM ENOS

PLUM CONSERVE
1 basket plums, 2 packages raisins, 12 oranges and grated peel, 2½ qts. sugar. Stone plums. Put all in kettle. Boi' slowly (simmer) till thick enough, 2 or 3 hours.
MRS. HATTIE A. WARDWELL

ORANGE FROSTING
1½ cups confectioner's sugar, butter size of walnut creamed with the sugar, a little of the orange rind grated into sugar, and mix with the orange juice to the right consistency.
MRS. GERTRUDE A. KING

Index

Archibald, Mrs. Everett H. 20, 32, 33, 41, 42
Bailey, Mrs. Joseph A. 35, 39
Baketel, Mrs. Roy V. 12, 14, 15, 37, 46
Bannister, Grace 38
Bannister, Winnifred 46
Barker, Mrs. 48
Barnes, Mrs. Carrie E. 6, 21, 46, 53
Barstow, Mrs. B.L. 11
Blodgett, Mrs. Geo. 18, 38
Bodwell, Mrs. J. W. 50
Brackett, Mrs. C. 20
Buswell, Mrs. Maude A. 10, 17, 18, 34, 41, 42, 44, 47, 54
Carleton, Mrs. C. A. 46
Carrow, Mrs. S. B. 6, 25, 47, 51, 52
Charnley, J. W. 47
Conant, Mrs. L.H. 3, 4, 17
Cook, Mrs. P. C. 8, 24
Crosby, Marion 13
Crowell, Mrs. A. C. 27
Davis, Mr. A. B. 9, 24, 25, 46
Dodge, Miss Florence 21, 27, 30, 37, 40, 41, 45, 52
Dodge, Mrs. H.A. 6, 42, 48
Dorwood, Mrs. M. E. 11
Douglas, Mrs Frank M. 20, 22, 47
Elphin, Mrs. W. K. 26
Emerson, Mrs. J. A. 5, 11, 27, 31, 39, 40, 53
Enos, Mrs. William 15, 23, 29, 31, 36, 43, 54
Fairfield, Miss 12
Fernald, Miss Maude 33
Fieldhouse, Susannah 39
Foster, Mildred A. 52
Foster, Mrs. Frederick W. 20, 50
Fraser, Dr. Agnes 5, 8, 53
Gabeler, Mrs. W. A. 11, 21, 24, 53
Gaunt, Mrs. Alfred 22, 35, 38, 52
Gaunt, Mrs. Henry 7, 16, 48
Gay, Mrs. Frederick 8
Goldsmith, Edith 4, 8, 14, 31
Goldsmith, Mrs. C. A. 13
Grant, Mrs. Harvey S. 16
Greene, Mrs. Amy 6, 20, 42
Hall, Mrs. Henry 32
Harrison, Mrs. Matthew 15, 43, 50
Hartshorne, Mrs. 21
Hastings, Mrs. Walter 24, 34, 43
Hayward, Mrs. Frederick D. 26, 28
Head, Mauld L. 50
Head, Mrs. S. C. 27
Heald, Mrs. A. E. 38
Health, Mrs. A. E. 19
High, Mrs. William 39
Hook, Mrs. Elizabeth 30, 43
Hook, Mrs. W. 37

Hutchins, Mrs. Warren 23, 32, 34, 35
Irish, Maude A. 3, 14, 28
Jager, Mrs. 29, 44
Jamieson, Mrs. M. 23
Jenkinson, Mrs. E. W. A.14, 36, 43, 54
Johnson, Mrs. Harry H. 6, 8, 38
Kay, Adelaide S. 13, 28
Kendall, Mrs. Charles. F. 30, 36, 37, 38
Kimball, Mrs. 21, 51
King, Mrs. Gertrude 12, 45, 46, 54
Libby, Mrs. Burton W 14, 31
Macdonald, Miss L. J. 33, 39
Mann, Mrs. Charles H. 45
Mann, Mrs. Susie J. 7, 18, 25, 52
Mikalson, Mrs. 33, 36, 46
Moore, Mrs. H. E. 5, 17, 18, 50
Morrison, Mrs. 19, 38
Morrison, Ruth 51
Morse, Miss 25
Nevins, Mrs. Harriet 22
Norris, Mrs. Rolf 4, 9, 43
Norris, Ruth 37, 51
Oliphant, Mrs. Charles H. 9, 16, 19, 26, 32, 49
Ostler, Mrs, John 23, 34
Paisley, Mrs. Wm O. 44, 49
Parker, Mrs. Henry 31
Parker, Mrs. J. O. 31
Putnam, Mrs. Leverett 29, 30
Rafferty, F. A. 52
Russell, Mrs. Charles E. 3, 29, 33, 45, 5
Sargent, Mrs. S.G. 17

Skinner, Mrs. 32
Smith, Mrs. 53
Smith, Mrs. Hugh 17, 35, 40, 47
Smith, Mrs. Stephen E. 6, 35, 48
Spence, Mrs. Clarence 23
Spicer, Mrs. 4, 6
Spooner, Mrs. Helen 5, 34
Stevens, Miss Hattie 40
Stowell, Mrs. Cyrus 13, 29
Swain Mrs. 7, 19
Swan, Mrs. 49
Tenney, Mrs. George 7, 10, 24, 36, 40, 41, 48
Thompson, Mrs. 15, 22, 49
Tripp, Marion H. 14
Tripp, Mrs. Thomas 13
Wagland, Mrs. A. H. 24
Wardwell, Mrs. Hattie A. 3, 4, 9, 12, 44, 54
Webster, Mrs. G. F. S. 33, 47
White, Mrs. Wallace 19, 34
Whittier, Jane 45
Woodbury, Mrs. D. D. 16, 35, 41, 42
Woodbury, Mrs. H. E. 18, 27, 39
Woodbury, Mrs. J.A. 11